31243 00 541 9246

Lake Forest Library
360 E. Deerpath
Lake Forest, IL 60045
847-234-0648
www.lakeforestlibrary.org

2/16

D1221880

Terry Fox

by Jennifer Sutoski

CAPSTONE PRESS
a capstone imprint

Pebble Plus is published by Capstone Press,
1710 Roe Crest Drive, North Mankato, Minnesota 56003
www.capstonepub.com

Copyright © 2016 by Capstone Press, a Capstone imprint. All rights reserved. No part of this publication may be reproduced in whole or in part, or stored in a retrieval system, or transmitted in any form or by any means, electronic, mechanical, photocopying, recording, or otherwise, without written permission of the publisher.

Library of Congress Cataloging-in-Publication Data
Cataloging-in-publication information is on file with the Library of Congress.

ISBN 978–1-4914-7836-3 (library binding : alk. paper)
ISBN 978–1-4914-7844-8 (pbk. : alk. paper)
ISBN 978–1-4914-7859-2 (eBook PDF)

Developed and Produced by Discovery Books Limited
Paul Humphrey: project manager
Sabrina Crewe: editor
Ian Winton: designer

Photo Credits
Gail Harvey/Bettmann/Corbis: cover, 9; Wikimedia Commons: title page, 7 (main image); Colin McConnell/Getty Images: 5; Dick Darrell/Toronto Star/Getty Images: 7 (inset); Boris Spremo/Toronto Star/Getty Images: 11; Bettmann/Corbis: 13, 17; David Cooper/Toronto Star/Getty Images: 15; CL Chang/Shutterstock: 19; Ralf Broskvar/Shutterstock: 21 (main image); Gwoeii/Shutterstock: 21 (top left); Kevin Hsieh/Shutterstock: 21 (bottom right).

Note to Parents and Teachers
The Canadian Biographies set supports national curriculum standards for social studies related to people and culture. This book describes and illustrates Terry Fox. The images support early readers in understanding text. The repetition of words and phrases helps early readers learn new words. This book also introduces early readers to subject-specific vocabulary words, which are defined in the Glossary section. Early readers may need assistance to read some words and to use the Table of Contents, Glossary, Read More, Internet Sites, and Index sections of the book.

Printed in China through World Print Ltd in 2015
007326WPF15

Table of Contents

Early Life

Terrance Stanley Fox was born
July 28, 1958, in Winnipeg,
Manitoba. He had two
brothers, Fred and Darrell,
and a sister, Judith.

born in Winnipeg,
Manitoba

1958

Terry with members of his family

At age 10, Terry moved to Port Coquitlam in British Columbia. Terry and his brothers loved many sports. They played road hockey and baseball. At high school and university, Terry played basketball.

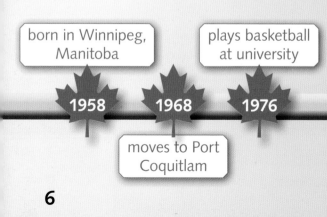

born in Winnipeg, Manitoba

plays basketball at university

1958

1968

1976

moves to Port Coquitlam

Terry pitching a baseball

The track and field at Terry's university

A Big Challenge

When Terry was 18, doctors told
him he had bone cancer. They
removed his right leg to stop the
cancer spreading. While he was
in hospital, Terry decided to
raise money for cancer research.

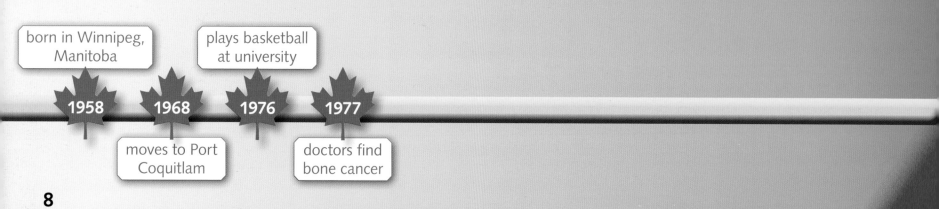

born in Winnipeg,
Manitoba

plays basketball
at university

1958   1968   1976   1977

moves to Port
Coquitlam

doctors find
bone cancer

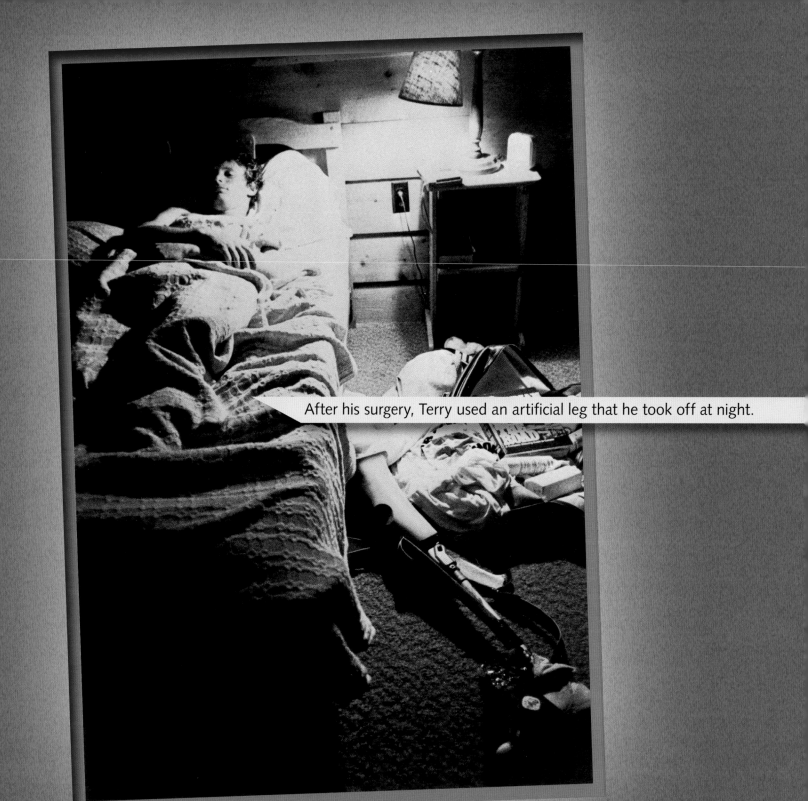

After his surgery, Terry used an artificial leg that he took off at night.

Terry started training for a long run in 1979. He wanted to run across Canada! Terry hoped to collect one dollar from every Canadian. The money would help to find a cure for cancer.

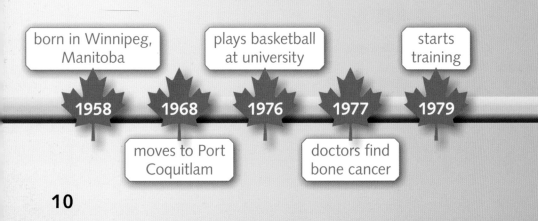

born in Winnipeg, Manitoba

plays basketball at university

starts training

1958   1968   1976   1977   1979

moves to Port Coquitlam

doctors find bone cancer

Terry wanted to help children with cancer, like this boy who came to watch him run.

Marathon of Hope

On April 12, 1980, Terry started his run in Newfoundland. He named it the "Marathon of Hope." He ran 5,300 kilometres to Ontario.

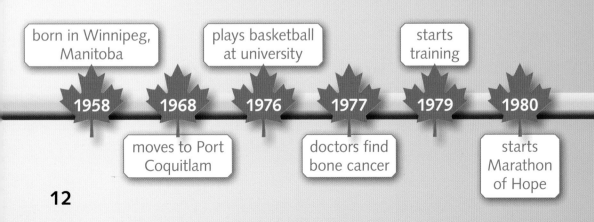

born in Winnipeg, Manitoba

plays basketball at university

starts training

1958   1968   1976   1977   1979   1980

moves to Port Coquitlam

doctors find bone cancer

starts Marathon of Hope

Terry runs along a busy road in Ontario.

Terry ran for 143 days. He became famous. On September 1, 1980, Terry had to stop. He was too sick to go on. Cancer had spread to his lungs.

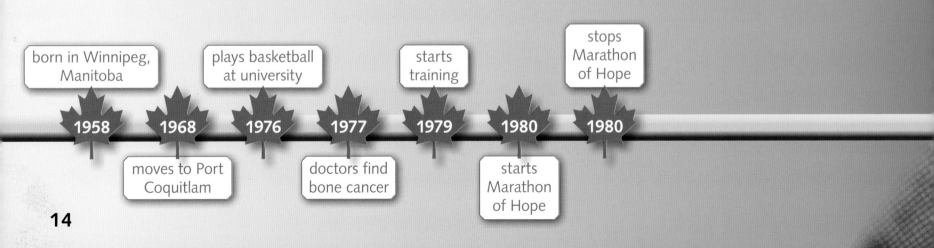

born in Winnipeg, Manitoba

1958

moves to Port Coquitlam

plays basketball at university

1968

1976

doctors find bone cancer

1977

starts training

1979

1980

starts Marathon of Hope

1980

stops Marathon of Hope

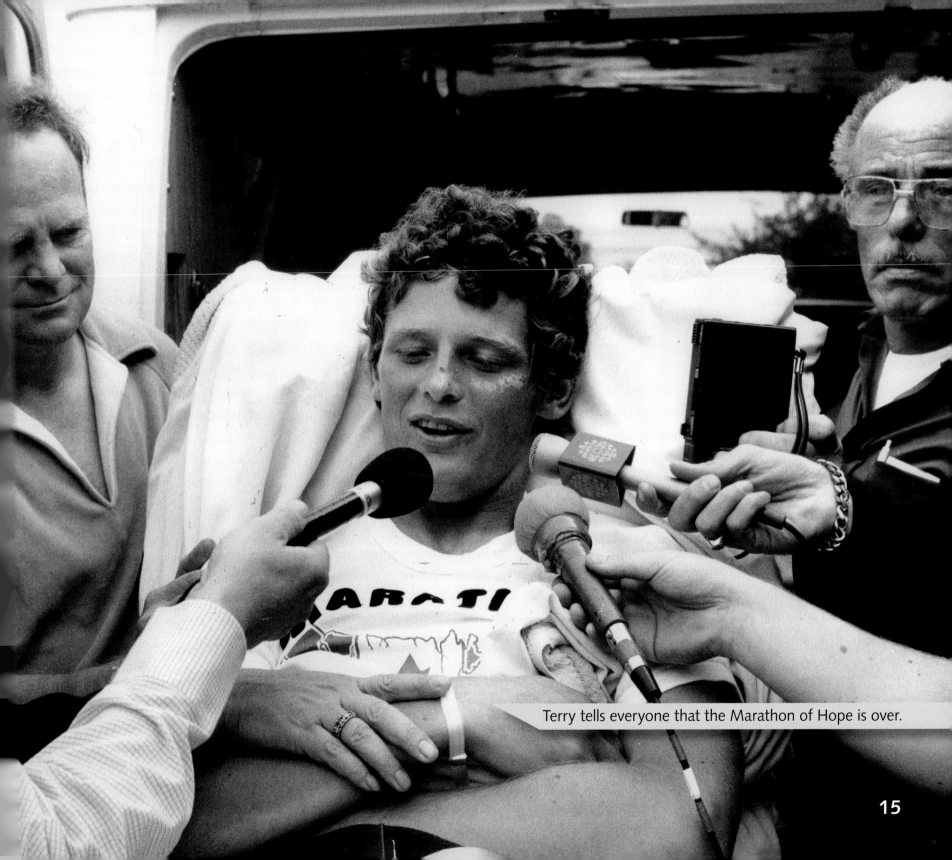

Terry tells everyone that the Marathon of Hope is over.

In February 1981, Terry achieved his dream. The Marathon of Hope raised 24 million dollars, one dollar for every Canadian. On June 29, 1981, Terry Fox died.

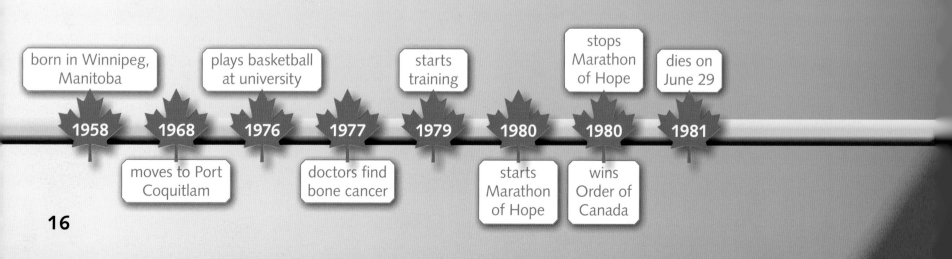

born in Winnipeg, Manitoba

plays basketball at university

starts training

stops Marathon of Hope

dies on June 29

1958 1968 1976 1977 1979 1980 1980 1981

moves to Port Coquitlam

doctors find bone cancer

starts Marathon of Hope

wins Order of Canada

Terry received the Order of Canada before he died. He is the youngest person ever to get the honour.

After Terry

Terry said, "Even if I don't finish, we need others to continue. It's got to keep going without me." The Marathon of Hope does keep going. People around the world run in memory of Terry.

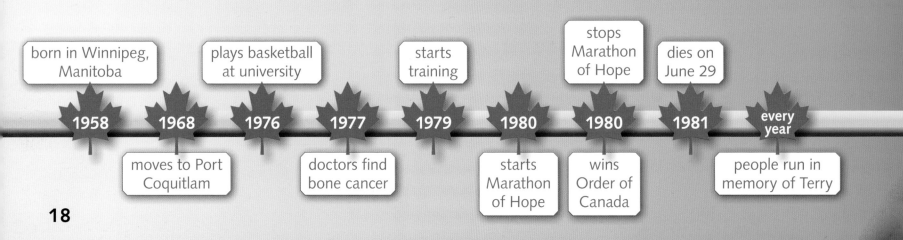

| 1958 | 1968 | 1976 | 1977 | 1979 | 1980 | 1980 | 1981 | every year |

born in Winnipeg, Manitoba

plays basketball at university

starts training

stops Marathon of Hope

dies on June 29

moves to Port Coquitlam

doctors find bone cancer

starts Marathon of Hope

wins Order of Canada

people run in memory of Terry

People in Malaysia warm up for a Terry Fox Run.

Terry Fox is a Canadian hero. People put up statues and name schools after him. Terry is on stamps and coins. Thanks to Terry, people give millions of dollars to cancer research.

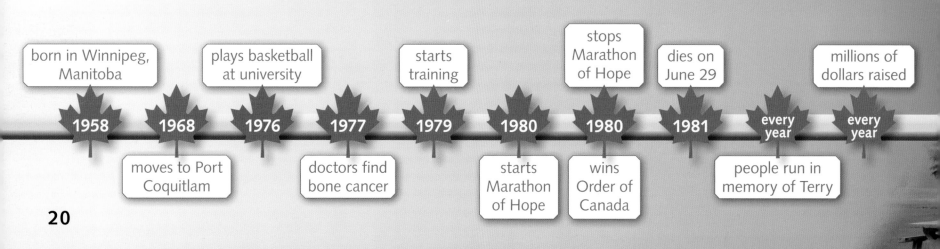

born in Winnipeg, Manitoba — 1958

moves to Port Coquitlam — 1968

plays basketball at university — 1968

doctors find bone cancer — 1977

starts training — 1979

starts Marathon of Hope — 1980

stops Marathon of Hope — 1980

wins Order of Canada — 1980

dies on June 29 — 1981

people run in memory of Terry — every year

millions of dollars raised — every year

This stamp shows Terry running his Marathon of Hope.

Mount Terry Fox in BC was named after Terry.

This statue is a memorial to Terry.

Glossary

artificial—something made to replace the real thing

cancer—a disease that starts from harmful cells growing
    inside a body

hero—a person who is admired, especially for being brave
    or doing good things

marathon—a very long run or race

memorial—something that helps us remember a person
    or event

Order of Canada—an award for very special Canadians

research—work people do to learn more about a problem
    so they can solve it

training—practising over and over to do something until
    you are ready

Read More

Trottier, Maxine. *Terry Fox: A Story of Hope*. Markham, ON: Scholastic Canada, 2005.

Manson, Ainslie. *Boy in Motion*. Vancouver, BC: Greystone Books, 2007.

Internet Sites

FactHound offers a safe, fun way to find Internet sites related to this book. All of the sites on FactHound have been researched by our staff.

Here's all you do:

Visit *www.facthound.com*

Type in this code: 9781491478363

 Check out projects, games and lots more at **www.capstonekids.com**

Index

Word Count: 268
Grade: 1
Early-Intervention Level: 17